PREACH
THE WORD

by
Billy Apostolon

BAKER BOOK HOUSE
Grand Rapids, Michigan

ISBN: 0-8010-0039-4

Eighteenth printing, May 1992

Printed in the United States of America

TO

— D A D D Y —

whose wise advice,

protecting love,

friendly criticism,

and

understanding heart,

whose remembrance

we shall always cherish,

this volume is

affectionately dedicated.

INTRODUCTION

One of the greatest disappointments in book buying has been in the field of sermon outlines. So often such a volume contains the self-evident and superficial. This present volume, *Preach the Word*, is different. I bespeak for it a wide sale and great usefulness. The distinctive characteristics which set Pastor Billy Apostolon's volume are these:

First, it is true to the Bible, thoroughly orthodox, basically fundamental, and doctrinally consistent.

Second, it is logically arranged, preserving a certain continuity of purpose and orderly sequence.

Third, while containing outlines that correlate the Scriptures on various subjects, it is simple enough to grip the interest and profound enough to challenge pursuance of the theme.

Fourth, these outlines are not only Scriptural but thoroughly practical and usable.

The "Seven Sevens" of sermons lend themselves not only to individual preaching upon certain topics, but also constitute an arrangement that fits well into a series of messages.

Pastor Apostolon has labored much in order to make accessible to busy pastors a wealth of usable material that safeguards from the by-path of secondary truth while containing a correlation of Scripture sufficient to guarantee Scriptural preaching.

We commend this volume to lovers of good sermon outlines, confident of their usefulness.

CHARLES H. STEVENS,
President of Piedmont Bible College,
Winston-Salem, North Carolina.

FOREWORD

In sending forth this series it is our prayer that the Lord may use them for His glory. We hope that this will not be just another series of sermon outlines, but that it may be a constant companion to the preacher of the Word. If this series can be used to the salvation of souls and the edification of the Church as the Lord's Servants "Preach the Bible as it is to People as They are," then one of the greatest purposes of our life will be fulfilled and the Lord Jesus may have all of the glory for whatever is accomplished in His Name.

May God's richest blessings be on you and yours as you continue to serve our Precious Saviour, the Lord Jesus Christ.

BILLY APOSTOLON

CONTENTS

I. The Seven Deadly Sins

PRIDE
PROVERBS 8:13

INTRODUCTION. *At the close of the sixth century, Pope Gregory the Great classified all sins under seven distinct sins. It was his view that all sins committed could be placed under one of the seven distinct sins. He said that these sins were pride, anger, envy, impurity, gluttony, slothfulness and avarice. From that time until the present these seven sins have been known as the "Seven Deadly Sins."*

I. WHAT IS PRIDE?
1. Pride is a sin; Prov. 21:4.
2. Pride is a sin that binds; Ps. 73:6.
3. Pride is an abomination to God; Prov. 16:5; Ps. 119:21.

II. FROM WHERE DOES PRIDE COME?
1. It comes from false wisdom; Rom. 1:22,28,29,30.
2. It comes from conceit; Prov. 26:12.
3. It comes from within; Mark 7:21,22.

III. WHEN DOES PRIDE BEGIN?
1. It begins with wealth . . . Hezekiah; II Kings 20:13; Isa. 39:2.
2. It begins with self-esteem . . . Haman; Esth. 5:11.
3. It begins with an exalted position . . . Naaman; II Kings 5:11-13.

IV. HOW DOES PRIDE AFFECT THE INDIVIDUAL?
1. It brings deception; Gal. 6:3.
2. It brings shame; Prov. 11:2.
3. It brings a man low; Prov. 29:23.

V. WHY IS PRIDE DANGEROUS?
1. It brings material loss . . . Nebuchadnezzar; Dan. 4:30,34; 5:20.
2. It brings punishment . . . Uzziah; II Chron. 26:16-19.
3. It leads to the condemnation of the Devil; I Tim. 3:6.

VI. HOW CAN PRIDE BE CURED?
1. By sober thinking; Rom. 12:3.
2. By humility; James 4:6; Phil. 2:3,5.
3. By the fear of the Lord; Ps. 111:10.

VII. WHAT HAPPENS WHEN PRIDE IS CURED?
1. The fruit of the Spirit will come; Gal. 5:22,23.
2. The love of the brethren will come; Eph. 4:1,2.
3. The instruction of others will come; II Tim. 2:25.

1

ANGER
PROVERBS 14:17

INTRODUCTION. *The words wrath and anger are closely related in meaning.*

I. WHAT IS ANGER?
1. Anger is a work of the flesh; Gal. 5:19,20.
2. Anger is a messenger of death; Prov. 16:14.
3. Anger is a sin that is hated by God; Amos 1:11.

II. FROM WHERE DOES ANGER COME?
1. It comes through grievous words; Prov. 15:1.
2. It comes through jealousy; Prov. 6:34.
3. It comes through the old nature (flesh); Gal. 5:19,20.

III. WHEN DOES ANGER BEGIN?
1. During a time of greed . . . Ahab toward Naboth; I Kings 21:4.
2. During a time of reproving . . . Asa toward the prophet; II Chron. 16:10.
3. During a time of arguing . . . Elihu toward his three friends; Job 32:3.

IV. HOW DOES ANGER AFFECT THE INDIVIDUAL?
1. It caused Cain to slay Abel; Gen. 4:5-8.
2. It caused the Jews to slay Stephen; Acts 7:54-59.
3. It caused Haman to conspire against Mordecai; Esth. 3:5.

V. WHY IS ANGER DANGEROUS?
1. It brings forth destruction; Col. 3:6.
2. It brings forth God's wrath; Rom. 1:18.
3. It brings hard feelings in the family; I Sam. 20:30-34.

VI. HOW CAN ANGER BE CURED?
1. By putting it off; Col. 3:8.
2. By refusing to do evil; Ps. 37:8.
3. By prayer; I Tim. 2:8. Prayer comes by knowing Christ.

VII. WHAT HAPPENS WHEN ANGER IS CURED?
1. A life of self-control will come; James 1:19.
2. A life of understanding will come; Prov. 14:29.
3. A life of fruit bearing will come; Col. 1:10,11.

ENVY
PROVERBS 27:4

INTRODUCTION. *In the English language the word envy is similar to jealousy.*

1. WHAT IS ENVY?
1. Envy is a sin that produces confusion; James 3:16.
2. Envy is a sin that kills; Job 5:2.
3. Envy is a sin of the rottenness of the bones; Prov. 14:30.

II. FROM WHERE DOES ENVY COME?
1. It comes from carnality; I Cor. 3:3.
2. It comes when there is unbelief; Acts 17:5.
3. It comes from a spirit of hatred; Matt. 20:24.

III. WHEN DOES ENVY BEGIN?
1. It begins when there is lust; Titus 3:3.
2. It comes when there is unbelief Acts 17:5.
3. It comes when God is forgotten; Rom. 1:28-32.

IV. HOW DOES ENVY AFFECT THE INDIVIDUAL?
1. It caused Joseph's brothers to hate him; Gen. 37:4,8,18-28.
2. It caused Saul to desire to kill David; I Sam. 18:7-11; 19:8-24.
3. It caused the Jews to speak against Paul's teachings; Acts 13:45.

V. WHY IS ENVY DANGEROUS?
1. It causes ill feelings . . . Prodigal's brother; Luke 15:25-32.
2. It brings confusion and evil work; James 3:14.
3. It brings hatred in the family; Gen. 37:4,8,11.

VI. HOW CAN ENVY BE CURED?
1. By manifesting love; I Cor. 13:4.
2. By putting on the Lord Jesus Christ; Rom. 13:13,14.
3. By living in the Spirit; Gal. 5:25,26.

VII. WHAT HAPPENS WHEN ENVY IS CURED?
1. The grudges of the past will be forgotten; James 5:9; Lev. 19:18.
2. The meekness toward all men will come; Titus 3:2-4.
3. The manifestation of love will be seen; I Cor. 13:4-7.

IMPURITY
REVELATION 22:15

INTRODUCTION. *In the English language the word for impurity is similar in meaning with unclean, filthy, sloppy, loathsome, nasty, repulsive, morally unfit and corrupt.*

I. WHAT ARE SOME KINDS OF IMPURITY?
1. Impurity of sex; Ex. 20:14.
2. Impurity in worship; Ex. 20:8,9,10.
3. Impurity in outward conduct; Ex. 20:7,13,15,16.

II. FROM WHERE DOES IMPURITY COME?
1. From within the individual; Mark 7:21.
2. From lust; Matt. 5:28.
3. From enticement; Prov. 9:13-18; II Tim. 3:6.

III. WHEN DOES IMPURITY BEGIN?
1. When there is a lack of understanding; Eph. 4:17-19.
2. When there is idleness . . . David; II Sam. 11:1-4.
3. When there is carnality; Rom. 8:7.

IV. HOW DOES IMPURITY AFFECT THE INDIVIDUAL?
1. It causes the individual to reap corruption; Gal. 6:7,8.
2. It causes death in the midst of life; I Tim. 5:6.
3. It causes the soul unrest; Isa. 57:20,21.

V. WHY IS IMPURITY DANGEROUS?
1. It caused Sodom and Gomorrah to be destroyed; Jude 7.
2. It causes death; I Cor. 10:8; Rom. 6:23.
3. It leads to Hell; Prov. 9:13-18.

VI. HOW CAN IMPURITY BE CURED?
1. By coming to the Lord; Matt. 11:28,29.
2. By the mortification of unclean members; Col. 3:5.
3. By confessing Christ; Rom. 10:9,10.

VII. WHAT HAPPENS WHEN IMPURITY IS CURED?
1. A pure conscience is experienced; II Tim. 1:3.
2. A fruitful life of holiness is experienced; I Thess. 4:7.
3. A zeal for good works is experienced; Titus 2:14.

GLUTTONY
DEUTERONOMY 21:20, 21

INTRODUCTION. *In the English language the word gluttony is similar in meaning with over-indulgence, in excess, selfishness and greed.*

I. WHAT IS GLUTTONY?
1. It is the sin of over-indulgence; Amos 6:4.
2. It is a sin that paints false pictures; Luke 12:19-36.
3. It is a sin that contaminates the body; I Cor. 6:19,20.

II. WHAT ARE THE TYPES OF GLUTTONY?
1. There is gluttony in eating; Prov. 30:21,22.
2. There is gluttony in drinking; Prov. 20:1.
3. There is gluttony in sinning; Luke 15:14.

III. FROM WHERE DOES GLUTTONY COME?
1. It comes from pride . . . Belshazzar; Dan. 5:1,2,27.
2. It comes from greed . . . Ananias and Sapphira; Acts 5:1,2.
3. It comes from covetousness . . . Ahab; I Kings 21:2-16.

IV. HOW DOES GLUTTONY AFFECT THE INDIVIDUAL?
1. It caused the Jews to lust after Egypt; Num. 11:4-6.
2. It caused Eli's sons to sin before God; I Sam. 2:12-17.
3. It caused the death of Belshazzar; Dan. 5:1,30.

V. WHY IS GLUTTONY DANGEROUS?
1. The glutton's belly becomes his god; Phil. 3:19.
2. The glutton forsakes the Lord's work; II Tim. 4:10.
3. The glutton's end is poverty; Prov. 23:21.

VI. HOW CAN GLUTTONY BE CURED?
1. By confessing the transgression; Ps. 32:5.
2. By seeking first the kingdom of God; Matt. 6:33.
3. By being filled with the Spirit; Eph. 5:18.

VII. WHAT HAPPENS WHEN GLUTTONY IS CURED?
1. A temperate life will be produced; Titus 1:7,8.
2. A saintly life will be produced; II Peter 1:5-8.
3. A life of fellowship will be produced; I Cor. 1:9.

SLOTHFULNESS
MATTHEW 20:6

INTRODUCTION. *In the English language the word slothfulness is similar in meaning with lazy, idle, neglectful, sluggish, inactive and laggard.*

I. WHAT IS SLOTHFULNESS?
1. It is refusing to work; Prov. 21:25.
2. It is a sin of being a "busybody"; I Tim. 5:13.
3. It is a sin of being disorderly; II Thess. 3:10-12.

II. FROM WHERE DOES SLOTHFULNESS COME?
1. It comes from ignorance; Isa. 56:10.
2. It comes from an idle life; Ezek. 16:49.
3. It comes from drowsiness; Prov. 23:21.

III. WHEN DOES SLOTHFULNESS BEGIN?
1. It begins when there is conceit; Prov. 26:16.
2. It comes when there is foolishness; Eccles. 4:5.
3. It comes when there is pride; Ezek. 16:49.

IV. HOW DOES SLOTHFULNESS AFFECT THE INDIVIDUAL?
1. It led the Jews to idolatry; Ex. 32:1-6.
2. It leads to begging during the harvest; Prov. 20:4.
3. It caused the 5 foolish virgins to be unprepared; Matt. 25:1-13.

V. WHY IS SLOTHFULNESS DANGEROUS?
1. It is the door to poverty; Prov. 20:13.
2. It causes hunger; Prov. 19:15.
3. It brings destruction; Eccles. 10:8.

VI. HOW CAN SLOTHFULNESS BE CURED?
1. By considering the way of work; Prov. 6:6-9.
2. By acknowledging the transgression; Ps. 51:2,3.
3. By occupying for Christ; Luke 19:13.

VII. WHAT HAPPENS WHEN SLOTHFULNESS IS CURED?
1. There will be the willingness to please Christ; II Tim. 2:2,3.
2. There will be the willingness to work for Christ; I Cor. 15:58.
3. There will be the willingness to occupy for Christ; I Cor. 3:6,7,8.

AVARICE
PROVERBS 21:26

INTRODUCTION. *In the English language the word avarice reveals a sin that is closely related to greed, stinginess, miserliness and covetousness.*

I. WHAT IS AVARICE?
1. It is a sin of idolatry; Col. 3:5.
2. It is a sin against God; Ex. 20:17.
3. It is a sin that causes trouble; Prov. 15:27.

II. WHAT IS THE EXTENT OF AVARICE?
1. It reaches from the prophet to the priest; Jer. 8:10.
2. It reaches to a king . . . King Saul; I Sam. 15:8,9.
3. It reaches from the least to the greatest; Jer. 6:13.

III. FROM WHERE DOES AVARICE COME?
1. It comes from self-love; II Tim. 3:2.
2. It comes from selfish desires; Matt. 25:8,9.
3. It comes from the heart; Mark 7:21.

IV. HOW DOES AVARICE AFFECT THE INDIVIDUAL?
1. It caused Felix to try to bribe Paul; Acts 24:26.
2. It caused Ahab to commit murder; I Kings 21:2-16.
3. It caused the rich young ruler to lose his soul; Luke 12:13-21.

V. WHY IS AVARICE DANGEROUS?
1. It causes some to err from the faith; I Tim. 6:10.
2. It causes a denial of God; Prov. 30:8,9.
3. It leads to an excuse for rejecting God's invitation; Luke 14:18.

VI. HOW CAN AVARICE BE CURED?
1. By setting the affections on Heavenly things; Col. 3:2-6.
2. By being content with what you have; Heb. 13:5.
3. By seeking God; Luke 12:22-31.

VII. WHAT HAPPENS WHEN AVARICE IS CURED?
1. There will be a renewed mind to use for God; Rom. 12:2.
2. There will be a walk worthy of God; I Thess. 2:12.
3. There will be holiness manifested before God; I Peter 3:11.

II. Seven Sermons to Saints
THE MASTER IS COME AND CALLETH FOR THEE
JOHN 11:28

I. THE MASTER CALLS TO SALVATION.
1. He calls the thirsty; John 7:37.
2. He calls the hungry; John 6:50,51.
3. He calls all who will come; Rev. 22:17.

II. THE MASTER CALLS TO SEPARATION.
1. He called Abraham to a separate life; Gen. 12:1.
2. He called Israel to separate from Egypt; Ex. 3:16,17.
3. He calls to separation with a promise; II Cor. 6:17,18.

III. THE MASTER CALLS TO FELLOWSHIP.
1. Fellowship is with the Father and Son; I John 1:3.
2. Fellowship is with other believers; Acts 2:42.
3. Fellowship is in the Name of Jesus; Matt. 18:20.

IV. THE MASTER CALLS TO SECURITY.
1. He gives security by the sealing of the Holy Spirit; Eph. 1:13.
2. He gives security through His Word; I John 5:12,13.
3. He gives security from the judgment; John 5:24.

V. THE MASTER CALLS TO SATISFACTION.
1. Satisfaction comes by knowing sins forgiven; I John 2:12.
2. Satisfaction comes by knowing we are children of God; Gal. 3:26.
3. Satisfaction comes by knowing we shall never perish; John 10:28,29.

VI. THE MASTER CALLS TO SERVICE.
1. The service is to God; I Cor. 10:31.
2. The service is witnessing; Acts 1:8.
3. The service should be continual; I Cor. 15:58.

VII. THE MASTER CALLS BELIEVERS TO ANOTHER SPHERE.
1. He has promised us a home in Heaven; John 14:1-3.
2. He has us looking forward to a home in Heaven; I Peter 1:4.
3. He will take us to our home in Heaven; I Thess. 4:13-18.

THE LAST WILL AND TESTAMENT OF OUR LORD JESUS
HEBREWS 9:16-22

I. A WILL MUST BE PUT ON RECORD.
  1. The Bible is recorded in Heaven; Ps. 119:89.
  2. The Bible is recorded to reveal Christ; John 20:31.
  3. The Bible was recorded to assure believers; I John 5:10-13.

II. A WILL MUST HAVE AN ADMINISTRATOR.
  1. The administrator must have wisdom; Col. 2:3.
  2. The administrator must have power; Matt. 28:18.
  3. The administrator must be present; Matt. 28:20.

III. A WILL MUST BE SIGNED BY THE TESTATOR.
  1. It was signed by His faultless life; Luke 23:4.
  2. It was signed byHis suffering; I Peter 4:12,13.
  3. It was signed by His resurrection; Rom. 4:25.

IV. A WILL REQUIRES WITNESSES.
  1. The Father is a witness; John 5:37,38.
  2. The Bible is a witness; John 5:39.
  3. The Holy Spirit is a witness; John 16:12-15.

V. A WILL IS NO GOOD WHILE THE TESTATOR LIVES.
  1. Jesus became man in order to die; Heb. 2:14.
  2. Jesus knew He had to die; Luke 9:30,31.
  3. Jesus' death is the Bible's theme; I Cor. 15:1,3,4.

VI. A WILL NAMES THE HEIRS.
  1. Paul tells us we are heirs; Gol. 4:7.
  2. Peter tells us we are heirs; I Peter 1:4.
  3. James tells us we are heirs; James 2:5.

VII. A WILL DESCRIBES THE INHERITANCE.
  1. A new nature; II Peter 1:4.
  2. A life of peace with God; Rom. 5:1.
  3. An inheritance in Heaven; I Cor. 2:9.

THE CHRISTIAN'S RACE
HEBREWS 12:1

I. THE CHRISTIAN'S RACE HAS A BEGINNING.
 1. It begins at the New Birth; John 3:3.
 2. It begins when the Christian offers himself; Rom. 12:1,2.
 3. It begins when a purging takes place; II Tim. 2:21.

II. THE CHRISTIAN'S RACE HAS RULES.
 1. It must be run with eyes on Christ; Heb. 12:2.
 2. It must be run with Heavenly affection; Col 3:2.
 3. It must be run with shod feet; Eph. 6:15.

III. THE CHRISTIAN'S RACE HAS A DEFINITE COURSE.
 1. It consists in contending for the faith; Jude 3.
 2. It consists in abounding in the Lord's work; I Cor. 15-58.
 3. It consists in holding forth the Word; Phil. 2:16.

IV. THE CHRISTIAN'S RACE HAS A GOAL.
 1. The goal is not to become a castaway; I Cor. 9:27.
 2. The goal is to fulfill our calling; Phil. 3:14.
 3. The goal is treasures in Heaven; Matt. 6:20.

V. THE CHRISTIAN RACE HAS A REGULAR SCHEDULE.
 1. It is to be run in this life; II Sam. 14:14.
 2. It is to be run during the day; John 9:4.
 3. It is to be run during the harvest; Luke 10:2.

VI. THE CHRISTIAN'S RACE HAS HINDRANCES.
 1. A hindrance is lack of faith; Matt. 14:31.
 2. A hindrance is lack of love; Luke 7:47.
 3. A hindrance is unconfessed sin; Rev. 2:5.

VII: THE CHRISTIAN'S RACE WILL BE REWARDED.
 1. An Incorruptible Crown for all runners; I Cor. 9:25.
 2. A Crown of Life for faithful Christians; Rev. 2:10.
 3. A Crown of Glory for faithful pastors; I Peter 5:4.

used

THE YIELDED LIFE
ROMANS 6:13

I. A CHRISTIAN'S EYES SHOULD BE YIELDED.
1. Yielded eyes will study the Bible; Ps. 1:2.
2. Yielded eyes will look to Jesus; Heb. 12:2.
3. Yielded eyes will look for the lost; John 4:35.

II. A CHRISTIAN'S EARS SHOULD BE YIELDED.
1. Yielded ears are deaf to gossip; I Tim. 4:7; 6:20.
2. Yielded ears are open to Jesus' Word; Luke 10:39.
3. Yielded ears are obedient to God's message; Acts 8:26,27.

III. A CHRISTIAN'S TONGUE SHOULD BE YIELDED.
1. A yielded tongue is bridled; James 1:26.
2. A yielded tongue is prayerful; I Tim. 2:1-4.
3. A yielded tongue will tell about Jesus; Mark 5:19,20.

IV. A CHRISTIAN'S HANDS SHOULD BE YIELDED.
1. Yielded hands do not steal; Eph. 4:28.
2. Yielded hands will help those in need; Heb. 12:12.
3. Yielded hands will make right the wrong; Acts 16:33.

V. A CHRISTIAN'S FEET SHOULD BE YIELDED.
1. Yielded feet are upon a rock; Ps. 40:2.
2. Yielded feet are shod with the gospel; Eph. 6:15.
3. Yielded feet will bruise Satan; Rom. 16:20.

VI. A CHRISTIAN'S HEART SHOULD BE YIELDED.
1. A yielded heart is clean; Ps. 51:10.
2. A yielded heart is Christ indwelled; Eph. 3:17.
3. A yielded heart will do God's will; Eph. 6:6.

VII. A CHRISTIAN'S WHOLE BODY SHOULD BE YIELDED.
1. A yielded body is God's workmanship; Eph. 2:10.
2. A yielded body is a sacrifice to God; Rom. 12:1.
3. A yielded body is the temple of the Holy Ghost; I Cor. 6:19.

THE EVIDENCE OF SALVATION
II CORINTHIANS 5:17; PHILIPPIANS 1:16

I. THE EVIDENCE IN THE SAMARITAN WOMAN'S LIFE.
1. She had feet that were in the Lord's service; John 4:28.
2. She witnessed concerning Christ; John 4:29.
3. She had a testimony that led people to Christ; John 4:39.

II. THE EVIDENCE IN THE GADARENE MANIAC'S LIFE.
1. He had a new nature; Luke 8:35; II Cor. 5:17.
2. He had a desire to follow Jesus; Luke 8:38.
3. He was commissioned to witness for Jesus; Luke 8:39.

III. THE EVIDENCE IN ZACCHAEUS' LIFE.
1. He received Christ joyfully; Luke 19:6.
2. He had an open heart to the poor; Luke 19:8a.
3. He desired to repent of his unrighteous life; Luke 19:8b.

IV. THE EVIDENCE IN THE ETHIOPIAN EUNUCH'S LIFE.
1. He confessed Christ; Acts 8:37.
2. He followed the Lord in Baptism; Acts 8:38.
3. He rejoiced in his salvation; Acts 8:39.

V. THE EVIDENCE IN THE PHILIPPIAN JAILOR'S LIFE.
1. He washed the preachers' stripes; Acts 16:33.
2. He showed kindness in his home to the prachers; Acts 16:34a.
3. He rejoiced in his salvation; Acts 16:34b.

VI. THE EVIDENCE IN THE APOSTLE PAUL'S LIFE.
1. He surrendered unto the Lord; Acts 9:6,18.
2. He preached Christ; Acts 9:20.
3. He became an ambassador for Christ; II Cor. 5:19,20.

VII. THE EVIDENCE THAT SHOULD BE IN THE BELIEVER'S LIFE.
1. The believer should keep the Word of God; Ps. 119:11,67.
2. The believer should have a forgiving spirit; Matt. 18:23-35.
3. The believer's life should be crucified; Gal. 2:20.

BLOCKADES TO SPIRITUAL BLESSINGS
PSALM 26:2

I. SELFISHNESS IS A BLOCKADE TO SPIRITUAL BLESSINGS.
1. Selfish people think only of themselves; Luke 12:17-19.
2. Selfish people show a lack of love; I John 3:17.
3. Selfish people reap what they sow; Acts 5:2,5,10.

II. LAZINESS IS A BLOCKADE TO SPIRITUAL BLESSINGS.
1. Lazy people beg in the harvest; Prov. 20:4.
2. Lazy people come to poverty; Prov. 6:9-11.
3. Lazy people will not work for Christ; Luke 19:20-24.

III. COVETOUSNESS IS A BLOCKADE TO SPIRITUAL BLESSINGS.
1. Covetousness troubles one's own house; Prov. 15:27.
2. Covetousness causes one to come to want; Prov. 22:16.
3. Covetousness brings God's judgment; Jer. 8:10.

IV. PRAYERLESSNESS IS A BLOCKADE TO SPIRITUAL BLESSINGS.
1. Prayerless people are troubled people; Dan. 9:13.
2. Prayerless people are disobedient people; Luke 18:1; James 4:2.
3. Prayerless people shall not prosper; Jer. 10:21.

V. WORLDLINESS IS A BLOCKADE TO SPIRITUAL BLESSINGS.
1. Worldliness reveals the inward life; I John 2:15.
2. Worldliness does not please God; Rom. 8:5-8.
3. Worldliness separates from God; James 4:4; Isa. 59:2.

VI. UNFRUITFULNESS IS A BLOCKADE TO SPIRITUAL BLESSINGS.
1. Unfruitfulness comes from not abiding in Christ; John 15:5.
2. Unfruitfulness results in the loss of reward; I Cor. 3:14,15.
3. Unfruitfulness brings judgment; Luke 19:20-26.

VII. UNFAITHFULNESS IS A BLOCKADE TO SPIRITUAL BLESSINGS.
1. Unfaithfulness is sin; Rom. 14:23.
2. Unfaithfulness robs of the Crown of Life; Rev. 2:10.
3. Unfaithfulness cannot please God; Heb. 11:6.

SEEK HIM
AMOS 5:8

I. SEEK HIM BECAUSE OF HIS OMNISCIENCE.
1. God knows our ways; Ps. 139:2,3.
2. God knows our words; Ps. 139:4.
3. God knows all things; I John 3:20.

II. SEEK HIM BECAUSE OF HIS OMNIPOTENCE.
1. He had power to create the universe; Gen. 1:1.
2. He has power to control nature; Ps. 107:25-27.
3. He has power to do everything; Job 42:2.

III. SEEK HIM BECAUSE OF HIS OMNIPRESENCE.
1. God is manifested everywhere; Jer. 23:23,24.
2. God's presence is known in Heaven and Hell; Ps. 139:7,8.
3. God's presence reaches to the uttermost sea; Ps. 139:9,10.

IV. SEEK HIM BECAUSE OF HIS HOLINESS.
1. God's holiness is seen in His hatred of sin; Prov. 15:9,26.
2. God's holiness is shown in His separation from sinners; Isa. 59:1,2.
3. God's holiness is shown in the punishment of the sinner; Ps. 5:4-6.

V. SEEK HIM BECAUSE OF HIS LOVE.
1. God loved us before we loved Him; I John 4:9,10.
2. God loves the sinner; Rom. 5:6-8.
3. God's love is seen in giving His Son; John 3:16.

VI. SEEK HIM BECAUSE OF HIS MERCY.
1. God's mercy is great; Ps. 145:8.
2. God's mercy is extensive; II Peter 3:9.
3. God's mercy is toward snners; Prov. 28:13.

VII. SEEK HIM BECAUSE OF HIS FORGIVENESS.
1. The Lord desires to forgive iniquity; Num. 14:18.
2. The Lord gives an invitation to forgiveness; Isa. 1:18.
3. The Lord forgives abundantly; Ps. 103:12.

III.   Seven Sermons to Sinners
FROM DISGRACE TO GRACE
TITUS 3:3-8

I.   MAN BY NATURE IS IN DISGRACE.
1.   His speech is a disgrace; Ps. 10:7.
2.   His walk is a disgrace; Prov. 6:18.
3.   His life is a disgrace; Col. 1:21.

II.   MAN BECAUSE OF HIS NATURE NEEDS SALVATION.
1.   He needs to be saved from his sin; Rom. 3:23.
2.   He needs to be saved from the law's curse; Gal. 3:10.
3.   He needs to be saved from God's wrath; Rom. 5:9.

III.   MAN'S MEANS OF CHANGING FROM DISGRACE TO GRACE.
1.   By the Word of God; I Peter 1:23.
2.   By the Holy Spirit; I Cor. 6:11.
3.   By coming to Jesus; John 6:37.

IV.   MAN CAN BE SAVED BY GRACE.
1.   Grace is sufficient; Acts 15:11.
2.   Grace is the means of forgiveness; Eph. 1:7.
3.   Grace is the means of justification; Titus 3:7.

V.   MAN'S JOY CHANGING FROM DISGRACE TO GRACE.
1.   He is a new man; Col. 3:10.
2.   He has a new standing; Rom. 5:1,2.
3.   He has a new position; II Cor. 5:20.

VI.   MAN NEEDS TO GROW IN GRACE.
1.   Growth comes by the study of the Bible; II Tim. 2:15.
2.   Growth comes by prayer; Luke 22:40.
3.   Growth comes by separation; I Thess. 5:21-23.

VII.   MAN IS KEPT BY GRACE.
1.   His hands are kept by grace; Eph. 4:28.
2.   His mouth is kept by grace; Ps. 40:3.
3.   His walk is kept by grace; Eph. 6:15.

GOD'S CURE FOR A SIN-SICK SOUL
MATTHEW 9:10-13

I. THE CAUSE OF A SIN-SICK SOUL.
1. The soul is sick because of disobedience; Rom. 5:19.
2. The soul is sick because of an inherited disease; Rom. 5:12.
3. The soul is sick because of a natural condition; Eph. 2:3.

II. THE CONDITION OF A SIN-SICK SOUL.
1. Deceitful in heart; Jer. 17:9.
2. Diseased from head to foot; Isa. 1:5,6.
3. Dead in trespasses and sins; Eph. 2:1; I Tim. 5:6.

III. THE CONSEQUENCES OF A SIN-SICK SOUL.
1. Sin separates from God; Isa. 59:2.
2. Sin brings forth death; Rom. 8:6; Ezek. 18:4.
3. Sin is incurable by human means; Prov. 20:9; Jer. 2:22; 13:23.

V. THE CONCERN FOR A SIN-SICK SOUL.
1. This is seen in God's mercy; Ps. 86:15.
2. This is seen in Christ's death; I Peter 3:18.
3. This is seen in the preacher's message; I Cor. 9:16; Rom. 1:15,16.

V. THE CONVICTION OF A SIN-SICK SOUL.
1. Conviction comes by the Word of God; Heb. 4:12.
2. Conviction comes by the Holy Spirit; John 16:8-11.
3. Conviction comes by the accusing conscience; Rom. 2:15.

VI. THE CURE OF A SIN-SICK SOUL.
1. Healing comes by the stripes of Jesus; I Peter 2:24.
2. Healing comes by repentance and faith; Acts 3:19; Heb. 11:6.
3. Healing comes immediately and is complete; Mark 1:42; Col. 2:9,10.

VII. THE CONFESSION OF A SIN-SICK SOUL.
1. Confession should be made of sin; Isa. 6:5; 64:6.
2. Confession should be made to the Lord; Ps. 51:1-4.
3. Confession reveals the belief of the heart; Rom. 10:9,10.

EXCUSES FOR NOT BEING SAVED AND GOD'S ANSWER
ROMANS 1:18-22

I. THE EXCUSES OF THE ATHEIST.
1. There is no God. God's answer; Ps. 14:1.
2. Science has the true answer. God's answer; I. Tim. 6:20; I Cor. 2:5.
3. Death is the end of man. God's answer; Heb. 9:27.

II. THE EXCUSES OF THE AGNOSTIC.
1. No one knows whether there is a God. God's answer; Ps. 19:1,2.
2. No one can know whether the Bible is true. God's answer; Ps. 119:89.
3. No one can know whether there is a Heaven. God's answer;
Matt. 10:32,33.

III. THE EXCUSES OF THE DECEIVED.
1. My way is all right. God's answer; Prov. 14:12.
2. I am living a good life. God's answer; James 2:10.
3. I am a church member. God's answer; John 3:3.

IV. THE EXCUSES OF THE UNCONVICTED.
1. I am not lost. God's answer; Rom. 3:23.
2. I don't have to believe. God's answer; John 3:18.
3. I don't have the feeling. God's answer; Isa. 55:1; Eph. 2:8,9.

V. THE EXCUSES OF THE CARELESS.
1. I am not living good enough to be saved. God's answer; Matt. 9:12,13.
2. I will become a Christian later. God's answer; Matt. 6:33.
3. I could not hold out. God's answer; II Tim. 1:12; II Peter 2:9.

VI. THE EXCUSES OF THE IGNORANT.
1. I have committed the unpardonable sin. God's answer; Rom. 10:13.
2. I can't give up my sins. God's answer; Gal. 6:7,8; John 8:36.
3. The Christian life is too hard. God's answer; Prov. 13:15.

VII. THE EXCUSES OF THE PROCRASTINATOR.
1. I will seek the Lord some other time. God's answer; Prov. 27:1.
2. I will be a Christian if my family agrees. God's answer; Mark 10:29,30.
3. There is plenty of time. God's answer; Matt. 25:10-12.

THE LAMB OF GOD
JOHN 1:29

I. THE LAMB PROPHESIED.
1. Moses prophesied concerning Him; Gen. 3:15; Num. 24:17.
2. Isaiah prophesied concerning Him; Isa. 53:4-12.
3. Jeremiah prophesied concerning Him; Jer. 23:5,6.

II. THE LAMB TYPIFIED.
1. He was typified by the Ark; Gen. 6:14.
2. He was typified by the Brazen Serpent; Num. 21:9.
3. He was typified by the Passover Lamb; Ex. 12:3-10.

III. THE LAMB PERSONIFIED.
1. His conception was by the Holy Spirit; Luke 1:34,35.
2. His body was prepared by the Father; Heb. 10:5.
3. His birth was by the Virgin Mary; Luke 2:7.

IV. THE LAMB MAGNIFIED.
1. He had power over disease; Mark 1:31.
2. He had power over devils; Mark 9:25-27.
3. He had power over death; Mark 5:41.

V. THE LAMB DESPISED.
1. He was despised by Herod; Matt. 2:8,16.
2. He was despised by the Jews; John 1:11; 19:14,15; Matt. 27:41-43.
3. He was despised by the governor's soldiers; Matt. 27:27-31.

VI. THE LAMB CRUCIFIED.
1. The blood of Christ atones; I Peter 1:18,19.
2. The blood of Christ preserves; Rom. 3:25.
3. The blood of Christ is sufficient; Heb. 2:9.

VII. THE LAMB GLORIFIED.
1. He was glorified to become our High Priest; Heb. 8:1.
2. He was glorified to become our Advocate; I John 2:1.
3. He was glorified to offer salvation; Heb. 7:25.

YOU CAN'T WIN AT THE GAME OF SIN
JAMES 1:15

I. CAIN PLAYED A LOSING GAME.
1. He worshipped God the wrong way; Gen. 4:3-5.
2. He slew his brother Abel; Gen. 4:8.
3. He became a vagabond on earth; Gen. 4:12.

II. THE ANTEDILUVIAN WORLD PLAYED A LOSING GAME.
1. The Antediluvian World was wicked; Gen. 6:5.
2. The Antediluvian World was warned; II Peter 2:5; Heb. 11:7.
3. The Antediluvian World perished; Gen. 7:21,23.

III. LOT'S WIFE PLAYED A LOSING GAME.
1. She knew she lived in a condemned city; Gen. 19:13,16.
2. She knew the way of deliverance; Gen. 19:17.
3. She disobeyed God and died; Gen. 19:26.

IV. HAMAN PLAYED A LOSING GAME.
1. He was King Ahasuerus' prime minister; Esth. 3:1.
2. He sought to destroy God's people; Esth. 3:6,8,9.
3. He was hanged on his own gallows; Esth. 7:9,10.

V. BELSHAZZAR PLAYED A LOSING GAME.
1. He was intemperate; Dan. 5:1.
2. He was immoral; Dan. 5:2.
3. He had his life taken away; Dan. 5:30.

VI. THE RICH FOOL PLAYED A LOSING GAME.
1. He was successful in material things; Luke 12:16.
2. He never included God in his plans; Luke 12:18,19.
3. He met sudden destruction; Luke 12:20.

VII. EVERY UNREPENTANT SINNER PLAYS A LOSING GAME.
1. His sin will find him out; Num. 32:23.
2. His sin must be reaped; Gal. 6:7,8.
3. His sin will pay the wages of death; Rom. 6:23.

used

THE BIBLE WAY OF SALVATION
GALATIANS 4:4, 5

I. THE FATHER'S POSITION IN SALVATION.
  1. God planned redemption; Gen. 22.
  2. God provided the Saviour; John 3:16,17.
  3. God did the reconciling; II Cor. 5:19.

II. THE SON'S POSITION IN SALVATION.
  1. He came to seek and save the lost; Luke 19:10.
  2. He came to give his life as a ransom; Matt. 20:28.
  3. He died for sinners; I Peter 1:18,19.

III. THE HOLY SPIRIT'S POSITION IN SALVATION.
  1. He convicts of sin; John 16:7,8.
  2. He regenerates the believer; Titus 3:5.
  3. He seals the believer; Eph. 4:30.

IV. THE BIBLE'S POSITION IN SALVATION.
  1. The Bible is necessary for faith; Rom. 10:17.
  2. The Bible searches the heart; Heb. 4:12.
  3. The Bible converts the individual; I Peter 1:23.

V. THE CHURCH'S POSITION IN SALVATION.
  1. The Church is commissioned with the gospel; Matt. 28:19,20.
  2. The Church is the guardian of the gospel; Jude 2,3.
  3. The Church is to send forth the gospel; Acts 1:8; 8:4.

VI. THE PREACHER'S POSITION IN SALVATION.
  1. He is God's watchman; Ezek. 33:7.
  2. He is to preach God's Word; II Tim. 4:2.
  3. He is to show sinners their transgression; Isa. 58:1.

VII. THE SINNER'S POSITION IN SALVATION.
  1. He must see his condition before God; Isa. 6:1,5.
  2. He must have faith in God; Heb. 11:6.
  3. He must receive Christ as his substitute; II Cor. 5:21.

THERE IS A GOD IN HEAVEN
DANIEL 2:28

I. MOSES KNEW THERE IS A GOD IN HEAVEN.
   1. God spoke to him from the burning bush; Ex. 3:2-6.
   2. God parted the Red Sea for him; Ex. 14:15-22.
   3. God communed with Moses on Sinai; Ex. 32:7,8.

II. JOSHUA KNEW THERE IS A GOD IN HEAVEN.
   1. God stopped the Jordan River for him; Josh. 3:13-17.
   2. God gave him the formula for taking Jericho; Josh. 6:1-20.
   3. God gave him the plan for the Cities of Refuge; Josh. 20.

III. DANIEL KNEW THERE IS A GOD IN HEAVEN.
   1. God revealed Nebuchadnezzar's dream to him; Dan. 2:19-30.
   2. God delivered his friends from the fiery furnace; Dan. 3:19-25.
   3. God delivered him from the lion's den; Dan. 16-24.

IV. ELISHA KNEW THERE IS A GOD IN HEAVEN.
   1. God took Elijah to Heaven from his presence; II Kings 2:11.
   2. God parted the Jordan River for him; II Kings 2:14.
   3. God brought blindness upon Syria's army; II Kings 6:18.

V. ISAAC KNEW THERE IS A GOD IN HEAVEN.
   1. God caused him to be born during his parents' old age; Gen. 21:2,3.
   2. God saved his life by providing a sacrifice; Gen. 22:1-19.
   3. God confirmed the Abrahamic covenant with him; Gen. 26:1-5.

VI. OUR LORD KNEW THERE IS A GOD IN HEAVEN.
   1. God spoke after His baptism; Matt. 3:16,17.
   2. God answered His prayer at Lazarus' grave; John 11:38-44.
   3. God raised Him from the dead; Rom. 10:9.

VII. THE SINNER SHOULD KNOW THERE IS A GOD IN HEAVEN.
   1. God knows the sinner's sins; Job 34:21-25.
   2. God punishes the sinner for his sins; Ps. 95:10,11.
   3. God offers forgiveness to the sinner; Isa. 55:7.

21

IV. Seven Sermons on Salvation
REGENERATION, A NEW LIFE FROM GOD
TITUS 3:5

I. THE MEANING OF REGENERATION.
   1. It means to become a new creature; II Cor. 5:17.
   2. It means to receive a Divine nature; II Peter 1:4.
   3. It means to have a spiritual quickening; Eph. 2:1.

II. THE NECESSITY OF REGENERATION.
   1. It is necessary because those in the flesh cannot please God; **Rom. 7:18.**
   2. It is necessary because our Lord demands it; John 3:7.
   3. It is necessary to enter into Heaven; Rev. 21:27.

III. THE MEANS OF REGENERATION.
   1. It is by the Word of God; I Peter 1:23; James 1:18.
   2. It is by the Holy Spirit; Titus 3:4,5.
   3. It is by faith in Christ; Acts 15:9; Gal. 3:26.

IV. THE PERSONS WHO CAN BE REGENERATED.
   1. The adulteress; John 8:1-11.
   2. The religious; Acts 9:4-6.
   3. Whosoever will receive Christ; I John 5:1.

V. THE PLACE WHERE REGENERATION OCCURS.
   1. The Philippian jailor was regenerated in jail; Acts 16:30-34.
   2. The Ethiopian was regenerated in the desert; Acts 8:37.
   3. The repentant thief was regenerated on the cross; Luke 23: 42,43.

VI. THE TIME WHEN REGENERATION OCCURS.
   1. Regeneration occurs when God's mercy is received; Titus 3:5.
   2. Regeneration occurs when faith is placed in Christ; John 3:14-16.
   3. Regeneration can occur now; Heb. 4:7.

VII. THE RESULTS OF REGENERATION.
   1. There is the indwelling of the Holy Spirit; I Cor. 3:16; 6:19.
   2. There is the transforming of the mind; Rom. 12:2.
   3. There is the assurance of everlasting life; Rom. 6:22.

FAITH, A NEW BELIEF IN G
HEBREWS 11:6

I. THE MEANING OF FAITH.
1. Faith is the assurance of things desired; Heb. 11:_.
2. Faith is taking God at His Word; John 5:24.
3. Faith is believing and trusting in God; Acts 27:25; Ps. 9:10.

II. THE NEED OF FAITH.
1. It is necessary to please God; Heb. 11:6.
2. It is necessary to obtain salvation; Eph. 2:8.
3. It is necessary to obtain assurance; I John 5:13.

III. THE MEANS OF FAITH.
1. It comes from the Word of God; Rom. 10:17.
2. It comes from our Lord Jesus; Heb. 12:2.
3. It comes from God the Father; Rom. 12:3.

IV. THE TRAGEDY OF NOT HAVING FAITH.
1. Unbelievers will die in their sins; John 8:24.
2. Unbelievers will not enter into God's rest; Heb. 3:19.
3. Unbelievers will spend eternity in Hell; Rev. 21:8.

V. THE HINDRANCES TO FAITH.
1. A hindrance is seeking man's glory; John 5:44.
2. A hindrance is an erring heart; Heb. 3:10,11.
3. A hindrance is Satan; Luke 8:12,18.

VI. THE TIME WHEN FAITH OCCURS.
1. Noah had faith when God warned him; Heb. 11:7; Gen. 6:22.
2. Jairus had faith when his daughter was sick; Mark 5:22,23.
3. The Ethiopian had faith when he heard of Jesus; Acts 8:37.

VII. THE CONSEQUENCE OF HAVING FAITH.
1. It produces knowledge of the remission of sins; Acts 10:43.
2. It produces a victorious life; Eph. 6:16; I John 5:4.
3. It produces the fearlessness of death; Jon 11:25-27.

REPENTANCE, A NEW MIND ABOUT GOD
ACTS 20:21

I. THE MEANING OF REPENTANCE.
1. It means to change the mind; Matt. 12:41.
2. It means to turn to God from evil; Acts 26:18; I Thess. 1:9.
3. It means to confess sin; Luke 15:21; Ps. 38:18.

II. THE IMPORTANCE OF REPENTANCE.
1. It was the message of John the Baptist; Matt. 3:1-10.
2. It was the message of our Lord; Matt. 4:17; Rev. 2,3.
3. It was the message of the Apostle Paul; Acts 17:30; 26:19,20.

III. THE NECESSITY OF REPENTANCE.
1. It is the direct command of God; Acts 17:30.
2. It is necessary to receive God's forgiveness; Acts 3:19.
3. It is the only way to escape destruction; Jonah 3:4,10.

IV. THE PLACE WHERE REPENTANCE CAN OCCUR.
1. Joseph's brethren repented in Egypt; Gen. 50:17,18.
2. Jonah repented in the whale's belly; Jonah 2:1-10.
3. The publican repented in the temple; Luke 18:13.

V. THE DANGER OF NEGLECTING REPENTANCE.
1. Those who don't repent ensnare themselves; Ps. 9:16.
2. Those who don't repent will perish; Luke 13:3,5.
3. Those who don't repent will be judged accordingly; John 12:48.

VI. THE TIME WHEN REPENTANCE CAN OCCUR.
1. Josiah repented when he heard the Word of God; II Kings 22:11.
2. David repented when rebuked by Nathan; II Sam. 12:10,13,16.
3. Repentance comes when there is hatred of sin; Job 42:5,6.

VII. THE EFFECT OF REPENTANCE.
1. It brings pardon; Isa. 55:7.
2. It brings forgiveness; Acts 3:19.
3. It brings Heavenly joy; Luke 15:7,10.

JUSTIFICATION, A NEW STATE BEFORE GOD
ACTS 13:39

I. THE MEANING OF JUSTIFICATION.
1. It means that sin is forgiven; Acts 13:38,39.
2. It means that there is no charge against the justified; Rom. 8:33,34
3. It means that there is complete restoration; Luke 15:21-24.

II. THE NEED OF JUSTIFICATION.
1. It is needed because of the world's guilt; Rom. 3:19.
2. It is needed because man has no righteousness; Isa. 64:6.
3. It is needed because of God's wrath on sin; John 3:36; Eph. 5:6.

III. THE MEANS OF JUSTIFICATION.
1. It is by the free gift of God's grace; Rom. 3:23,24.
2. It is by the blood of Christ; Rom. 5:9.
3. It is by faith in Jesus Christ; Rom. 5:1.

IV. THE PERSONS WHO CAN BE JUSTIFIED.
1. Those who come and reason with God; Isa. 1:18.
2. Those who confess their sins; Ps. 32:5.
3. Those who are willing to receive Christ Jesus; Rom. 8:1.

V. THE EXTENT OF JUSTIFICATION.
1. Justification reaches to the religious; Acts 18:8.
2. Justification reaches to idol worshippers; I Thess. 1:9,10.
3. Justification reaches to those in poverty; Luke 16:22.

VI. THE TIME WHEN JUSTIFICATION OCCURS.
1. Abraham was justified as soon as he believed God; James 2:23.
2. Abel was justified when he offered a bloody sacrifice; Heb. 11:4.
3. Justification comes immediately by faith; Rom. 4:5.

VII. THE BLESSINGS OF JUSTIFICATION.
1. There is peace with God; Rom. 5:1.
2. There is a new relationship with God; Titus 3:7.
3. There is deliverance from God's wrath; Rom. 5:9

ADOPTION, A NEW RELATIONSHIP WITH GOD
I JOHN 3:1

I. THE MEANING OF ADOPTION.
1. It means the placing of a son; Ex. 2:10; Acts 7:21.
2. It means receiving a place in a family; Esth. 2:7.
3. It means to belong to a new household; Eph. 2:19.

II. THE MEANS OF ADOPTION.
1. Adoption was planned by God the Father; Gal. 4:4,5.
2. Adoption is made possible by Jesus Christ; Eph. 1:5.
3. Adoption comes by the Word of God; James 1:18.

III. THE PLACE WHERE ADOPTION CAN OCCUR.
1. Zacchaeus was adopted under a sycamore tree; Luke 19:4-6.
2. Paul was adopted on the way to Damascus; Acts 9:4-6.
3. Lydia was adopted at a prayer meeting; Acts 16:14,15.

IV. THE TIME WHEN ADOPTION OCCURS.
1. Adoption comes when the gospel is received; I John 5:9,10.
2. Adoption comes when God's love is accepted; I John 4:10; Luke 14:17.
3. Adoption is hindered by procrastination; Acts 17:32.

V. THE CONDITIONS UNDER WHICH ADOPTION OCCURS.
1. There must be an invitation to be adopted; Luke 18:16.
2. There must be a separation from evil; II Cor. 6:17,18.
3. There must be a personal reception of Christ; John 1:12.

VI. THE REASON WHY SOME ARE NOT ADOPTED.
1. Adoption is hindered by Satan; Luke 8:12.
2. Adoption is hindered by rebellion; Acts 7:54.
3. Adoption is hindered by procrastination; Acts 17:32.

VII. THE JOY THAT COMES BY BEING ADOPTED.
1. The adopted are called God's sons; I John 3:1.
2. The adopted are joint heirs with Christ; Rom. 8:17.
3. The adopted will dwell in the Father's house; John 14:2,3.

ASSURANCE, A NEW BLESSING FROM GOD
JOHN 10:28, 29

I. THE MEANING OF ASSURANCE.
1. It means the believer has security; John 10:28,29.
2. It means the knowledge of eternal life; I John 5:12,13.
3. It means there is knowledge of being God's child; I John 3:1-3.

II. THE NECESSITY OF ASSURANCE.
1. It is necessary to know the forgiveness of sins; I Peter 2:24.
2. It is necessary to please God; Heb. 11:5,6.
3. It is necessary when facing life; Rom. 8:38,39.

III. THE MEANS OF ASSURANCE.
1. Assurance comes by the Holy Ghost; Eph. 4:30; I John 5:10.
2. Assurance comes by believing on the Son; John 3:36.
3. Assurance comes by the Word of God; John 5:24.

IV. THE PERSONS WHO CAN HAVE ASSURANCE.
1. Those who are kings . . . David; Ps. 23:4-6.
2. Those who are suffering persecution . . . Job; Job 19:25-27.
3. Those who are believers in Christ . . . Paul; II Tim. 1:12.

V. THE TRAGEDY OF NOT HAVING ASSURANCE.
1. Without assurance there is no peace; Col. 3:15.
2. Without assurance there is no blessedness; Ps. 32:1,2.
3. Without assurance there can be no true witnessing; Acts 8:35.

VI. THE TIME WHEN ASSURANCE COMES.
1. It comes when the gosepl is understood; Col. 2:2; I Thess. 1:5.
2. It comes when there is faith; Heb. 10:22.
3. It comes when God's Word is kept; I John 2:5.

VII. THE JOY THAT COMES WITH ASSURANCE.
1. Assurance produces the knowledge of Christ's presence; Matt. 28:20.
2. Assurance produces the fearlessness of death; John 11:26.
3. Assurance produces the certainty of the resurrection; Ps. 17:15.

SANCTIFICATION, A NEW LIFE BEFORE GOD
I THESSALONIANS 4:3

I. THE MEANING OF SANCTIFICATION.
1. It means to be set apart for God; Rom. 12:1,2.
2. It means to have a holy life; Lev. 20:7.
3. It means to have a yielded life; Rom. 6:19.

II. THE NECESSITY OF SANCTIFICATION.
1. It is necessary to see God. Heb. 12:14.
2. It is necessary to grow in the Lord; I Peter 2:2,3.
3. It is necessary to please God; Lev. 11:44; I Thess. 4:1.

III. THE MEANS OF SANCTIFICATION.
1. Sanctification comes from God; I Thess. 5:23; Jude 1.
2. Sanctification comes by the Holy Spirit; II Thess. 2:13; I Peter 1:2.
3. Sanctification comes by the Word; John 17:17; 15:3.

IV. THE PERSONS WHO CAN BE SANCTIFIED.
1. The Jews; I Chron. 15:12-14.
2. The Gentiles; Rom. 15:16.
3. The Church; Eph. 5:25,26.

V. THE TIME WHEN SANCTIFICATION OCCURS.
1. Sanctification is instantaneous; Heb. 10:10.
2. Sanctification is progressive; II Peter 3:18.
3. Sanctification will be complete when Christ returns; I John 3:2.

VI. THE EVIDENCE OF SANCTIFICATION.
1. There is a departure from the wicked; I Cor. 5:11.
2. There is a desire for worship; Ps. 122:1; Heb. 10:25.
3. There is a life of purity; Ps. 119:9,11; I Tim. 5:22.

VII. THE BLESSINGS OF SANCTIFICATION.
1. The sanctified are blessed with forgiveness; Acts 26:18.
2. The sanctified are in unity with Christ; Heb. 2:11.
3. The sanctified have a perfected position before God; Heb. 10:14.

V. Seven Sermons for Funerals
GOOD NEWS AT THE HOUR OF DEATH
JOHN 11:38-44

I. THE CROSS OF CALVARY IS GOOD NEWS.
1. Calvary gives news of a finished redemption; John 19:30.
2. Calvary gives news of forgiveness; Luke 23:34.
3. Calvary gives news of salvation; Luke 23:43.

II. THE OPPORTUNITY OF LIFE IS GOOD NEWS.
1. Life gives the opportunity of being a Christian; John 1:12.
2. Life gives the opportunity of living for Jesus; John 14:23.
3. Life gives the opportunity of everlasting life; John 5:24.

III. THE INSEPARABLE LOVE OF GOD IS GOOD NEWS.
1. God loved us while we were sinners; Rom. 5:8.
2. God loved us with mercy; Eph. 2:4.
3. God loves us with an inseparable love; Rom. 8:38,39.

IV. THE RESURRECTION IS GOOD NEWS.
1. We look forward to the resurrection: Job 19:25-27.
2. We shall be resurrected by God's power; I Cor. 6:14.
3. We shall be satisfied with the resurrection; Ps. 17:15.

V. THE BELIEVERS' REUNION IS GOOD NEWS.
1. We shall dwell with Old Testament Saints; Matt. 8:11.
2. We shall dwell with New Testament Saints; I Thess. 4:17.
3. We shall dwell with Christ; Col. 3:4.

VI. THE COMFORT OF GOD IS GOOD NEWS.
1. God comforts us by spiritual blessings; Eph. 1:3.
2. God comforts us by His keeping power; Ps. 37:28.
3. God comforts us by His promises; I Chron. 28:20.

VII. THE ASSURANCE OF HEAVEN IS GOOD NEWS.
1. Heaven is promised to us; John 14:1-3.
2. Heaven is reserved for us; I Peter 1:4.
3. Heaven is our eternal dwelling place; Ps. 23:6.

WHAT YOUR LIFE IS
JAMES 4:14

I. LIFE IS A GIFT FROM GOD.
  1. God is the author of life; Gen. 2:7.
  2. God holds the issues of life; Ps. 68:20.
  3. God sustains life; Ps. 121:8.

II. LIFE OFFERS A CHALLENGE.
  1. There is a challenge to receive Jesus; John 1:12.
  2. There is a challenge to serve Jesus; Luke 9:23.
  3. There is a challenge to do good to all men; Gal. 6:10.

III. LIFE HAS ITS JOY.
  1. There is joy when a sinner comes home; Luke 15:6.
  2. There is joy in worshipping Christ; Luke 24:52.
  3. There is joy in suffering for Christ; Acts 16:25.

IV. LIFE HAS ITS SORROW.
  1. Job became wearied with life; Job 10:18-20.
  2. Elijah became wearied with life; I Kings 19:4.
  3. Jonah became wearied with life; Jonah 4:8,9.

V. LIFE IS BRIEF.
  1. Life is like a vapor; James 4:14.
  2. Life is like a shadow; I Chron. 29:15.
  3. Life is but a step this side of death; I Sam. 20:3.

VI. LIFE ON EARTH CAN BE EXTENDED.
  1. By honoring parents; Ex. 20:12; Deut. 5:16.
  2. By keeping God's commandments; Deut. 4:40.
  3. By respecting nature; Deut. 22:6,7.

VII. LIFE CAN BE EVERLASTING.
  1. Jesus came that life could be abundant; John 10:10.
  2. Jesus gives everlasting life; John 10:28.
  3. Jesus assures of everlasting life; Phil. 1:6.

THE DEATH OF A GREAT LEADER
JOSHUA 1:2

I. THE BIRTH OF A GREAT LEADER.
1. He was born of faithful parents; Heb. 11:23.
2. He was born during a time of trial; Ex. 1:11,16.
3. He was born for a purpose; Ex. 2:10.

II. THE CHOICE OF A GREAT LEADER.
1. He chose to be unyoked with Egypt; Heb. 11:25.
2. He chose to suffer for God; Heb. 11:25.
3. He chose to live by faith; Heb. 11:27-29.

III. THE VISION OF A GREAT LEADER.
1. He had a vision of the burning bush; Ex. 3:2-6.
2. He had a vision of God's power; Ex. 14:21,22.
3. He had a vision of the Promised Land; Deut. 34:1.

IV. THE CONTACT WITH GOD OF A GREAT LEADER.
1. God revealed His plan to him; Ex. 3:7-10.
2. God commissioned him; Ex. 3:16,17.
3. God gave him power; Ex. 11:3.

V. THE PROMISE TO A GREAT LEADER.
1. He was promised God's presence; Ex. 3:12.
2. He was promised God's instruction; Ex. 4:11,12.
3. He was promised victory; Ex. 3:10,17.

VI. THE WORK OF A GREAT LEADER.
1. He had a message from God; Ex. 7:2.
2. He worked as God's deliverer; Ex. 12:31,32.
3. He worked to deliver God's commandments; Ex. 34:4; 35:1.

VII. THE DEATH OF A GREAT LEADER.
1. He died at 120 years; Deut. 34:7.
2. He died after being a blessing; Deut. 33:1-3.
3. He died according to God's plan; Deut. 34:5.

\VEN, THE HOME UP ABOVE
JOHN 14:2

_PARED HOME.

__ ~~ a place prepared by Jesus; John 14:2.
2. It is a city prepared by God; Heb. 11:10,16.
3. It is a place for prepared people; Rev. 21:27.

II. HEAVEN IS A PERFECT HOME.
1. It is free from the wicked; Gal. 5:21.
2. It is free from the unclean; Eph. 5:5.
3. It will be marvelous in nature; I Cor. 2:9.

III. HEAVEN IS AN ETERNAL HOME.
1. It is an eternal home for believers; II Cor. 5:1.
2. It is a home of eternal occupation; Rev. 22:3,4.
3. It is a home of eternal beauty; Rev. 21:2.

IV. HEAVEN IS A HAPPY HOME.
1. It is a place of no sorrow; Rev. 21:4.
2. It is a place of no sin; Rev. 21:27.
3. It is a place of rest from labors; Rev. 14:13.

V. HEAVEN IS AN INHABITED HOME.
1. Heaven is inhabited by God the Father; Dan. 7:13; Mark 11:25,26.
2. Heaven is inhabited by Christ; Heb. 8:1; Acts 7:55.
3. Heaven is inhabited by the Redeemed; Rev. 5:9.

VI. HEAVEN IS A DESIRED HOME.
1. Because our names are written there; Luke 10:20.
2. Because our inheritance is there; I Peter 1:4.
3. Because we will be united with Christ; I Thess. 4:17.

VII. HEAVEN IS AN ACCESSIBLE HOME.
1. Heaven is accessible by Christ; John 14:6.
2. Heaven is accessible by faith; Heb. 11:6.
3. Heaven is accessible by conversion; Matt. 18:3.

THE STEP OF DEATH
I SAMUEL 20:3

I. THE STEP OF DEATH IS A UNIVERSAL STEP.
1. It is appointed to man to die; Heb. 9:27.
2. All mankind is subject to death; Ps. 49:10.
3. The living know that they shall die; Eccles. 9:5.

II. THE STEP OF DEATH IS A NEAR STEP.
1. Age is nothing before God; Ps. 39:4,5.
2. Life appears only for a little while; James 4:14.
3. Man's days are like a shadow; Ps. 144:4.

III. THE STEP OF DEATH IS AN UNCERTAIN STEP.
1. We have no continuing city here; Heb. 13:14.
2. We know not the day of death; Gen. 27:2.
3. We shall be cut off as a flower; James 1:10,11.

IV. THE STEP OF DEATH IS A SEPARATING STEP.
1. It separates a mother from her son; Luke 7:12.
2. It separates a father from his son; II Sam. 12:22,23.
3. It separates sisters from their brother; John 11:21,32.

V. THE STEP OF DEATH IS A MOTIVATING STEP.
1. It motivates a faithful life; Rev. 2:10.
2. It motivates a yielded life; Rom. 6:13.
3. It motivates a Christ-centered life; Col. 1:18.

VI. THE STEP OF DEATH CAN BE A BLESSED STEP.
1. It can be to a blessed country; Heb. 11:16.
2. It can be to a blessed position; Rev. 14:13.
3. It can be to a blessed condition; I John 3:1.

VII. THE STEP OF DEATH CAN BE A PREPARED STEP.
1. Christ is able to give eternal life; Heb. 7:25.
2. Christ gives eternal life to all believers; John 11:25,26.
3. Christ gives security to all believers; I John 5:11-13.

BLESSED ASSURANCE, JESUS IS MINE
II TIMOTHY 1:12

I.   JESUS IS OUR ASSURANCE IN PRAYER.
1.   He has given us the pattern for prayer; Luke 11:1,2.
2.   He wants us to pray in His name; John 14:14.
3.   He is able to answer our prayer; Eph. 3:20.

II.   JESUS IS OUR ASSURANCE IN TEMPTATION.
1.   He is able to keep us from falling; Jude 24.
2.   He will give us victory over temptation; I Cor. 10:13.
3.   He will reward us for resisting temptation; James 1:12.

III.   JESUS IS OUR ASSURANCE OF GUIDANCE.
1.   He is our ever present Guide; Heb. 13:5.
2.   He guides us by the Bible; Ps. 119:105.
3.   He guides us through His Spirit; Rom. 8:14.

IV.   JESUS IS OUR ASSURANCE OF ETERNAL LIFE.
1.   He is the Author and Finisher of our faith; Heb. 12:2.
2.   He is the Shepherd and Bishop of our souls; I Peter 2:25.
3.   He gives us eternal life; John 10:28,29.

V.   JESUS IS OUR ASSURANCE IN DEATH.
1.   He has the keys of death; Rev. 1:18.
2.   He gives comfort in death; Ps. 23:4.
3.   He takes the sting out of death; I Cor. 15:55-57.

VI.   JESUS IS OUR ASSURANCE IN THE RESURRECTION.
1.   We shall be resurrected because of Him; II Cor. 4:14.
2.   We shall have a new body; Phil. 3:20,21.
3.   We shall be like Him; I John 3:2.

VII.   JESUS IS OUR ASSURANCE OF HEAVEN.
1.   We have desired Heaven; Heb. 11:16.
2.   We have an inheritance in Heaven; I Peter 1:4.
3.   We will be taken to Heaven by Him; I Thess. 4:16,17.

THE DEAD IN CHRIST
I THESSALONIANS 4:16

I. THE DEAD IN CHRIST HAVE A PURCHASED LIFE.
1. Their life has been purchased with a great price; I Cor. 7:23.
2. Their life has been purchased with Christ's blood; I Peter 1:18,19.
3. Their life has been purchased for a purpose; I Cor. 12:27.

II. THE DEAD IN CHRIST HAVE AN ETERNAL SALVATION.
1. Eternal salvation is promised by Christ; John 6:51.
2. Eternal salvation was made known by Paul; Phil. 1:6.
3. Eternal salvation was assured by the Apostle John; I John 5:13.

III. THE DEAD IN CHRIST HAVE A LIFE THAT GLORIFIES GOD.
1. God is glorified by their walk; I John 2:6.
2. God is glorified by their talk; Col. 3:17.
3. God is glorified by their complete life; Rom. 6:13.

IV. THE DEAD IN CHRIST ARE GOD'S MESSENGERS.
1. It is a message backed by God's power; Rom. 1:16.
2. It is a message backed by God's presence; Matt. 28:19,20.
3. It is a message by God's ambassador; II Cor. 5:20.

V. THE DEAD IN CHRIST WILL BE CHANGED.
1. The dead Saints will be resurrected; I Thess. 4:16.
2. The living Saints will be changed; I Cor. 15:51,52.
3. The changed Saints will be like Christ; I John 3:1-3.

VI. THE DEAD IN CHRIST HAVE A HOME IN HEAVEN.
1. It is a prepared home; John 14:3.
2. It is a reserved home; I Peter 1:4.
3. It is a happy home; Rev. 21:4.

VII. THE DEAD IN CHRIST WILL BE REWARDED.
1. The reward will be to those who labor for Christ; Ps. 126:6.
2. The Lord will reward after He comes; II Tim. 4:8.
3. The Lord will reward personally; Rev. 22:12.

VI. Seven Sermons about the Saviour
THE CRUCIFIED CHRIST
MATTHEW 27:33-50

I. THE CRUCIFIXION WAS PROPHESIED.
   1. It was prophesied by Isaiah; Isa. 53:2-12.
   2. It was prophesied by Daniel; Dan. 9:26.
   3. It was prophesied by Zechariah; Zech. 13:6.

II. THE CRUCIFIXION WAS NOT DESERVED.
   1. He knew no sin; II Cor. 5:21.
   2. He did no sin; I Peter 2:22.
   3. He was without sin; Heb. 4:15.

III. THE CRUCIFIXION WAS VOLUNTARILY.
   1. He came to give His life as a Ransom; Matt. 20:28.
   2. He was led as a lamb to the slaughter; Isa. 53:7.
   3. He gave Himself as a sacrifice to God; Eph. 5:2.

IV. THE CRUCIFIXION WAS SHAMEFUL.
   1. He was crucified on a tree; Gal. 3:13.
   2. He was crucified in the midst of mockery; Mark 15:18-20.
   3. He was crucified by His own nation; Acts 2:23.

V. THE CRUCIFIXION CAUSED AGONY.
   1. Agony came because of the crown of thorns; Matt. 27:29.
   2. Agony came when He was forsaken by the Father; Matt. 27:46.
   3. Agony came when He suffered thirst; John 19:28.

VI. THE CRUCIFIXION WAS SUBSTITUTIONARY.
   1. The Just took the place of the unjust; I Peter 3:18.
   2. The Sinless took the place of the sinner; II Cor. 5:21.
   3. The Guiltless was made a curse for us; Gal. 3:13.

VII. THE CRUCIFIXION OF CHRIST WAS VICTORIOUS.
   1. By His crucifixion we are reconciled to God; Rom. 5:10.
   2. By His crucifixion He conquered death; Rev. 1:18.
   3. By His crucifixion we have a gospel to preach; I Cor. 15:3,4.

THE CHANGELESS CHRIST
HEBREWS 13:8

I.   CHRIST IS CHANGELESS IN HIS WISDOM.
1.   He is the wisdom of God; I Cor. 1:24.
2.   He was filled with wisdom from His youth; Luke 2:40.
3.   He has wisdom that astonishes men; Matt. 13:54.

II.   CHRIST IS CHANGELESS IN HIS HOLINESS.
1.   He knew no sin; II Cor. 5:21.
2.   He was without sin in His life; Heb. 4:15.
3.   He abides in a life of faithfulness; II Tim. 2:13.

III.   CHRIST IS CHANGELESS IN HIS LOVE.
1.   He died to prove His love; Eph. 5:2.
2.   He manifests love in cleansing from sin; Rev. 1:5.
3.   He gives us love that is inseparable; Rom. 8:35-39.

IV.   CHRIST IS CHANGELESS IN HIS POWER.
1.   He has power over all flesh; John 17:2.
2.   He had power to overcome the world; John 16:33.
3.   He had power to ascend into Heaven; Eph. 4:8.

V.   CHRIST IS CHANGELESS IN HIS PROMISES.
1.   His promise of eternal life is changeless; John 11:25.
2.   His promise of another Comforter was changeless; Luke 24:49; Acts 2.
3.   His promise of His personal return is changeless; John 14:1-3.

VI.   CHRIST IS CHANGELESS IN HIS GOSPEL INVITATION.
1.   His gospel invitation is extended by the Holy Spirit; Rev. 22:17.
2.   His gospel invitation is to a prepared feast; Luke 14:17.
3.   His gospel invitation is to all; Matt. 11:28.

VII.   CHRIST IS CHANGELESS IN HIS ABILITY TO SAVE.
1.   He is the only way to Heaven; John 14:6.
2.   He is the only person who can save; Acts 4:12.
3.   He has the ability to forgive sins; Luke 7:48,49.

THE CHALLENGING CHRIST
JOHN 6:37

I. CHRIST OFFERS A CHALLENGE TO THE HUNGRY.
1. He challenges the hungry to come; Matt. 22:4.
2. He challenges the hungry to come without price; Isa. 55:1.
3. He challenges to a life free from hunger; John 6:35.

II. CHRIST OFFERS A CHALLENGE TO THE THIRSTY.
1. He challenges the thirsty with everlasting life; John 4:14.
2. He challenges the thirsty with life indwelling; John 7:38.
3. He challenges the thirsty by the church; Rev. 22:17.

III. CHRIST OFFERS A CHALLENGE TO THE WEARY.
1. He challenges the weary to come to Him; Matt. 11:28.
2. He challenges with the promise of peace; John 14:27; 16:33.
3. He challenges with the promise of eternal rest; Rev. 14:13.

IV. CHRIST OFFERS A CHALLENGE TO THE BACKSLIDER.
1. He challenges the backslider to repent; II Chron. 7:14.
2. He challenges a return to the first love; Rev. 2:4,5.
3. He challenges with a promise of forgiveness; I John 1:9.

V. CHRIST OFFERS A CHALLENGE TO YOUNG PEOPLE.
1. He challenges them to remember God; Eccles. 12:1.
2. He challenges them to come to Him; Matt. 19:14.
3. He challenges them to live for Him; Phil. 1:21.

VI. CHRIST OFFERS A CHALLENGE TO HIS SAINTS.
1. He challenges them to witness; Matt. 28:19,20; Acts 1:8.
2. He challenges them to pray; Matt. 7:7; Luke 18:1.
3. He challenges them to surrender their lives; Rom. 12:1,2.

VII. CHRIST OFFERS A CHALLENGE TO PREACHERS.
1. He challenges the preacher to study the Word; II Tim. 2:15; 3:14-17.
2. He challenges the preacher to preach the Word; II Tim. 4:1-4.
3. He challenges the preacher to a consecrated life; I Tim. 6:11,12.

THE CURING CHRIST
LUKE 7:21

I. CHRIST'S CURE WAS AVAILABLE TO THE DEMON POSSESSED.
  1. He cured the demon possessed in Capernaum; Mark 1:23-26.
  2. He cured the Maniac of Gadara; Mark 5:8-13.
  3. He cured the demon possessed boy; Luke 9:37-42.

II. CHRIST'S CURE WAS AVAILABLE TO LEPERS.
  1. He healed the man full of leprosy; Luke 5:12-15.
  2. He healed ten lepers at once; Luke 17:14.
  3. He gave His disciples power to heal lepers; Matt. 10:8.

III. CHRIST'S CURE WAS AVAILABLE TO THE LAME.
  1. He cured the man with the withered hand; Mark 3:1-6.
  2. He cured the woman with the infirmity; Luke 13:10-13.
  3. He used His power in healing the lame man; Acts 3:6-8.

IV. CHRIST'S CURE WAS AVAILABLE TO THE BLIND.
  1. He healed blind Bartimaeus; Mark 10:52.
  2. He healed the blind man of Bethsaida; Mark 8:22-26.
  3. He healed the man blind from birth; John 9:7.

V. CHRIST'S CURE WAS AVAILABLE TO THE HELPLESS.
  1. Christ cured the impotent man; John 5:7-11.
  2. Christ cured the palsied man; Luke 5:18-26.
  3. Christ, the Good Samaritan, cured the helpless man; Luke 10:30-35.

VI. CHRIST'S CURE WAS AVAILABLE TO THE DEAD.
  1. He gave life to the dead son of the Widow of Nain; Luke 7:11-17.
  2. He gave life to Jairus' Daughter; Luke 8:51-56.
  3. He gave life to Lazarus; John 11:41-44.

VII. CHRIST'S CURE IS AVAILABLE TO THE UNSAVED.
  1. He is the only offering for sin; Heb. 10:18.
  2. He has the power to forgive sins; Luke 5:24.
  3. He cures the sinner satisfactorily; I Cor. 6:11.

THE CONQUERING CHRIST
HEBREWS 12:2

I. CHRIST WAS A CONQUEROR IN LIFE.
1. He was filled with wisdom as a child; Luke 2:46-47.
2. He was obedient in His life; Luke 2:49; 22:42.
3. He was undefiled in life; Heb. 7:25,26.

II. CHRIST WAS A CONQUEROR OVER DISEASE.
1. He healed the woman with the issue of blood; Matt. 9:20-22.
2. He healed the deaf man with the speech impediment; Mark 7:32-37.
3. He healed Peter's mother-in-law of her fever; Luke 4:38,39.

III. CHRIST WAS A CONQUEROR OVER NATURE.
1. He turned the water into wine; John 2:7-10.
2. He calmed the stormy sea; Luke 8:22-25.
3. He caused the fig tree to be fruitless; Matt. 21:18-20.

IV. CHRIST WAS A CONQUEROR OVER SATAN.
1. He was prophesied to conquer Satan; Gen. 3:15.
2. He conquered Satan during the temptation; Luke 4:1-13.
3. He gave His life to eternally conquer Satan; Heb. 2:14; Rev. 20:10.

V. CHRIST WAS A CONQUEROR OVER DEATH.
1. He was resurrection from the dead; Luke 24:5,6; Rom. 1:4.
2. He has the keys to hell and death; Rev. 1:18.
3. He is a living Saviour at God's right hand; Heb. 12:2.

VI. CHRIST WAS A CONQUEROR AT CALVARY.
1. He forgave His persecutors at Calvary; Luke 23:34.
2. He saved the repentant thief on Calvary; Luke 23:42,43.
3. He finished the plan of salvation on Calvary; John 19:30: I Tim. 1:15.

VII. CHRIST WILL BE A CONQUEROR AT HIS SECOND COMING.
1. He will resurrect the dead Saints; I Cor. 15:52.
2. He will deliver believers from death's grave; I Cor. 15:54.
3. He will change both the dead and living Saints; I Cor. 15:51-53.

THE COMFORTING CHRIST
II THESSALONIANS 2:16, 17

I. CHRIST IS A DIVINE COMFORTER.
  1. He was recognized as a Teacher from God; John 3:2.
  2. He was equal with God; Phil. 2:5-8; John 10:30-39.
  3. He was God in the flesh; I Tim. 3:16.

II. CHRIST IS A QUALIFIED COMFORTER.
  1. He was prophesied as a qualified comforter; Isa. 35:4-6.
  2. He is qualified to comfort all afflictions; Matt. 11:5.
  3. He is qualified to comfort because of His creative acts; Col. 1:16.

III. CHRIST IS A PERFECT COMFORTER.
  1. He is perfect in knowledge; John 1:48; 2:24,25.
  2. He was perfect in His behavior; I Peter 2:21-24.
  3. He was perfect in the offering He made; Heb. 10:10-14.

IV. CHRIST IS A LIVING COMFORTER.
  1. He lived to bring comfort to Simeon; Luke 2:25-32.
  2. He lived to bring comfort to Mary Magdalene; John 20:11-18.
  3. He lived to comfort His disciples; John 20:19-23.

V. CHRIST IS AN ETERNAL COMFORTER.
  1. He is the same yesterday, today and forever; Heb. 13:8.
  2. He is ever in the midst of believers; Matt. 18:20.
  3. He is ever present to comfort; Matt. 28:20.

VI. CHRIST IS A FORGIVING COMFORTER.
  1. He has the authority to forgive sins; Luke 5:20-24.
  2. He came into the world to forgive sinners; Luke 19:10.
  3. He forgave Peter and commissioned him; Matt. 26:69-75;
                                                    John 21:15-17.

VII. CHRIST IS AN INTERCEDING COMFORTER.
  1. He is interceding at the right hand of God; Rom. 8:34.
  2. He is interceding to forgive the sins of believers; I John 1:9.
  3. He is interceding desiring to see souls saved; Heb. 7:25.

41

THE COMING CHRIST
ACTS 1:11

I. THE COMING OF CHRIST IS PROMISED.
1. Christ promised that He would come; John 14:1-3.
2. Angels promised that He would come; Acts 1:11.
3. Paul promised that He would come; Heb. 10:37.

II. THE COMING OF CHRIST IS PREACHED.
1. The Apostle John preached it; I John 3:2.
2. The Apostle Peter preached it; Acts 3:20.
3. The Apostle James preached it; James 5:7.

III. THE COMING OF CHRIST IS PLANNED.
1. It is planned to be the Blessed Hope; Titus 2:11-13.
2. It is planned to be the Purifying Hope; I John 3:3.
3. It is planned to be the Comforting Hope; I Thess. 4:18.

IV. THE COMING OF CHRIST IS FOR A PURPOSE.
1. He is coming to fulfill His promise; John 14:28.
2. He is coming to receive His Church; Acts 15:14; John 14:1-3.
3. He is coming to reward the faithful; Luke 12:42-44.

V. THE COMING OF CHRIST IS WITH POWER.
1. He is to come in His Father's glory; Matt. 16:27.
2. He is to come in the angels' glory; Luke 9:26.
3. He is to come in His own glory; Matt. 24:30.

VI. THE COMING OF CHRIST HAS A PATTERN.
1. There will be a sound from Heaven; I Thess. 4:16.
2. There will be a change in the dead and living Saints; I Cor. 15:52-54.
3. There will be a reunion with Christ; I Thess. 4:16,17.

VII. THE COMING OF CHRIST SHOULD BE PREPARED FOR.
1. It should be prepared for by repentance; Ps. 38:18.
2. It should be prepared for by receiving Christ; John 10:9.
3. It should be prepared for by living for Christ; I Thess. 5:6.

VII. Seven Sermons for Special Occasions
NEW YEAR'S DAY
NEW THINGS FOR THE NEW YEAR
II CORINTHIANS 5:17

I. A NEW FAITH.
1. A faith centered in Christ; Heb. 12:2.
2. A faith that works for Christ; James 2:17.
3. A faith to live for Christ; Heb. 10:38.

II. A NEW POSITION.
1. A position on the Rock; Ps. 40:2.
2. A position of acceptance; Eph. 1:6.
3. A position of no condemnation; Rom. 8:1.

III. A NEW ASSURANCE.
1. An assurance over doubt; John 10:28.
2. An assurance over temptation; Rev. 3:10.
3. An assurance forever; Ps. 121:8.

IV. A NEW SERVICE.
1. A cross-bearing life; Luke 14:27.
2. A self-denying life; Matt. 16:24.
3. A Christ-following life; Mark 8:34.

V. A NEW JOY.
1. Joy because of deliverance; Col. 1:13.
2. Joy because of liberty; Gal. 5:13.
3. Joy because of comfort; Ps. 23:4.

VI. A NEW PRAYER LIFE.
1. A prayer for our enemies; Matt. 5:44.
2. A prayer for all in authority; I Tim. 2:1,2.
3. A prayer that is steadfast; I Thess. 5:17.

VII. A NEW TESTIMONY.
1. A testimony of praise; Ps. 119:171.
2. A testimony as lights in the world; Matt. 5:14.
3. A testimony without sin; Job 2:10.

GOOD FRIDAY
SEVEN CRIES FROM CALVARY
JOHN 7:46

I. THE CRY OF FORGIVENESS; Luke 23:33,34.
1. It was prophesied; Isa. 53:12.
2. It was backed by power; Matt. 9:6.
3. It is extensive; Col. 2:13.

II. THE CRY OF SALVATION; Luke 23:42.
1. It proves salvation is by grace; Eph. 2:8,9.
2. It proves salvation is by Christ; I Tim. 2:5.
3. It proves salvation comes instantly; Rom. 10:9,10,13.

III. THE CRY OF PROVISION; John 19:26,27.
1. It shows the compassion of Christ; Luke 7:13.
2. It manifests Christ's obedience; Ex. 20:12.
3. It sets forth an example; Eph. 6:1,2.

IV. THE CRY OF DESERTION; Matt. 27:46.
1. It reveals Christ's love for mankind; John 15:13.
2. It reveals God's holiness; Hab. 1:13.
3. It reveals God's plan of salvation; II Cor. 5:21.

V. THE CRY OF SUFFERING; John 19:28.
1. It was prophesied; Ps. 69:21.
2. It reveals Christ's humanity; Luke 2:51.
3. It reveals Christ's pain; Ps. 69:3; Isa. 53:5.

VI. THE CRY OF VICTORY; John 19:30.
1. It shows salvation's plan was finished; Heb. 7:27.
2. It shows the Father's work was finished; John 6:38.
3. It shows Christ's suffering was finished; Heb. 12:2.

VII. THE CRY OF DEATH; Luke 23:46.
1. It reveals Christ's yielded life; Matt. 26:39.
2. It reveals Christ's obedience; Phil. 2:8.
3. It reveals Christ's power; John 10:15,17,18.

44

EASTER

WHAT CHRIST'S RESURRECTION MEANS TO MANKIND
I CORINTHIANS 15:1-4

I. IT MEANS THAT WE HAVE PROOF THAT CHRIST DIED.
1. Proof by His broken body; John 20:27.
2. Proof that sin has been punished; Isa. 53:5.
3. Proof that Christ was made a curse for us; Gal. 3:13.

II. IT MEANS THAT GOD WAS SATISFIED WITH CHRIST'S DEATH.
1. God resurrected Christ by His power; Eph. 1:19,20.
2. God resurrected Christ to His right hand; Acts 5:30,31.
3. God by the resurrection proves Christ's Sonship; Rom. 1:4.

III. IT MEANS THAT PROPHECY WAS FULFILLED.
1. David prophesied the resurrection; Ps. 16:9,10.
2. The resurrection was promised to the Fathers; Acts 13:32,33.
3. Christ prophesied the resurrection; Matt. 20:19.

IV. IT MEANS THAT WE HAVE A GOSPEL TO PREACH.
1. It was the theme of Paul's gospel; II Tim. 2:8.
2. It is the basis of the gospel; I Cor. 15:14,17.
3. It is important in the plan of salvation; Rom. 10:9.

V. IT MEANS THAT WE CAN BE JUSTIFIED BEFORE GOD.
1. Justification is based on Christ's resurrection; Rom. 4:25.
2. Justification brings no condemnation; Rom. 8:1.
3. Justfication brings peace; Rom. 5:1.

VI. IT MEANS THAT WE HAVE A HIGH PRIEST IN HEAVEN.
1. A High Priest at God's right hand; Heb. 10:12.
2. A High Priest that makes intercession for us; Heb. 7:25.
3. A High Priest that is preparing a place for us; John 14:2.

VII. IT MEANS THAT BELIEVERS HAVE LIFE AFTER DEATH.
1. Christ has the keys to Hell and death; Rev. 1:5,18.
2. Christ's resurrection assures us of the resurrection; II Cor. 4:14.
3. Christ's resurrection assures believers of Heaven; I Peter 1:3,4.

MOTHER'S DAY
THE INFLUENCE OF MOTHERS
I TIMOTHY 5:14

I. MOTHERS SHOULD INFLUENCE WITH PRAYER, LIKE HANNAH.
1. Hannah was childless; I Sam. 1:5,6.
2. Hannah prayed for a child; I Sam. 1:10,11.
3. Hannah's prayer was answered; I Sam. 1:19,20.

II. MOTHERS SHOULD INFLUENCE WITH DEVOTION, LIKE RUTH.
1. She was devoted to Naomi; Ruth 1:16,17.
2. She gleaned in Boaz's field; Ruth 2:3.
3. She was rewarded for her devotion; Ruth 4:13,21,22.

III. MOTHERS SHOULD BE INTERESTED IN THE WORD,
LIKE MARY.
1. She heard the Word at Jesus' feet; Luke 10:39.
2. She chose a good part in loving the Word; Luke 10:42.
3. She saw the Word in action; John 11:43,44.

IV. MOTHERS SHOULD INFLUENCE BY DECISIONS,
LIKE REBEKAH.
1. Her decision was the right decision; Gen. 24:58.
2. Her decision proved a blessing; Gen. 24:67.
3. Her decision was for life; Gen. 49:31.

V. MOTHERS SHOULD INFLUENCE BY FAITH, LIKE THE
QUEEN OF SHEBA.
1. Through faith she heard; I Kings 10:1.
2. Through faith she came; I Kings 10:2.
3. Through faith she witnessed; I Kings 10:7.

VI. MOTHERS SHOULD INFLUENCE WITH AN OPEN HEART,
LIKE LYDIA.
1. Her heart was open to a prayer service; Acts 16:13.
2. Her open heart heard the gospel; Acts 16:14.
3. Her open heart opened her home; Acts 16:15.

VII. MOTHERS SHOULD INFLUENCE IN WORSHIP, LIKE THE
WOMAN OF CANAAN.
1. She worshipped the right person; Matt. 15:22.
2. She worshipped in a time of need; Matt. 15:25.
3. She was rewarded for her worship; Matt. 15:28.

FATHER'S DAY
THE INFLUENCE OF FATHERS
ISAIAH 38:19

I. FATHERS SHOULD INFLUENCE WITH PRAYER, LIKE PAUL.
1. He knew the person of prayer; Eph. 3:11,12.
2. He knew how to pray; I Thess. 5:17.
3. He depended on prayer; I Thess. 5:25.

II. FATHERS SHOULD INFLUENCE WITH OBEDIENCE,
LIKE JOSHUA.
1. He was obedient in his report of the land of Canaan; Num. 14:6-9.
2. He was obedient in crossing the Jordan; Josh. 3:13-17.
3. He was obedient in conquering Jericho; Josh. 6:3-5,20.

III. FATHERS SHOULD INFLUENCE WITH PURITY, LIKE JOSEPH.
1. He was a goodly person; Gen. 39:6.
2. He resisted temptation; Gen. 39:12.
3. He exchanged kindness for hatred; Gen. 37:28; 42:16.

IV. FATHERS SHOULD INFLUENCE WITH PATIENCE, LIKE JOB.
1. Job had patience when he lost his family; Job 1:21.
2. Job had patience when he lost his health; Job 2:9,10.
3. Job had patience that ended in reward; Job 42:12-17.

V. FATHERS SHOULD INFLUENCE WITH FAITH, LIKE ABRAHAM.
1. By faith Abraham left Ur of the Chaldees; Heb. 11:8.
2. By faith Abraham journeyed to Canaan; Heb. 11:9.
3. By faith Abraham offered Isaac; Heb. 11:17.

VI. FATHERS SHOULD INFLUENCE WITH DECISIONS,
LIKE MOSES.
1. Moses chose against being Pharaohs' daughters' son; Heb. 11:24.
2. Moses chose against sin; Heb. 11:25.
3. Moses chose against Egypt's treasures; Heb. 11:26.

VII. FATHERS SHOULD INFLUENCE WITH A VISION, LIKE NOAH.
1. Noah's vision was of a perishing world; Gen. 6:13.
2. Noah's vision was of a way of escape; Heb. 11:7.
3. Noah's vision brought him safety; Gen. 8:16.

THANKSGIVING
GIVING THANKS AT THANKSGIVING
PSALM 92:1-4

I. WE SHOULD GIVE THANKS FOR OUR SAVIOUR.
1. For His devotion to the Father; Luke 22:42.
2. For His finished work; John 19:30.
3. For His saving power; John 6:37.

II. WE SHOULD GIVE THANKS FOR THE HOLY SPIRIT.
1. For His convicting power; John 16:8-11.
2. For His leadership; Rom. 8:14.
3. For His producing fruit in us; Gal. 5:22,23.

III. WE SHOULD GIVE THANKS FOR THE BIBLE.
1. For its inspiration; II Tim. 3:16.
2. For its power; Heb. 4:12.
3. For its message; John 3:16.

IV. WE SHOULD GIVE THANKS FOR SALVATION.
1. For the forgiveness of sin; Jer. 33:8.
2. For cleansing from sin; I John 1:9.
3. For the assurance of salvation; II Tim. 1:12.

V. WE SHOULD GIVE THANKS FOR THE CHURCH.
1. For its mission; Matt. 28:19,20.
2. For its position; Matt. 16:18.
3. For its eternal glory; Eph. 2:7.

VI. WE SHOULD GIVE THANKS FOR THE PROVISIONS OF LIFE.
1. For food; Rom. 14:6.
2. For faith; Rom. 1:8.
3. For answered prayer; I John 5:14,15.

VII. WE SHOULD GIVE THANKS FOR HEAVEN.
1. For our treasures that are there; Matt. 6:20.
2. For our names that are there; Luke 10:20.
3. For our home that is there; II Cor. 5:1.

CHRISTMAS

WHAT THE BIRTH OF CHRIST MEANS TO MANKIND
GALATIANS 4:4

I. IT MEANS PROPHECY WAS FULFILLED.
1. Prophecy fulfilled concerning place of birth; Micah 5:2; Luke 2:4.
2. Prophecy fulfilled concerning means of birth; Isa. 7:14; Matt. 1:23.
3. Prophecy fulfilled concerning lineage; Gen. 22:18; Matt. 1:1.

II. IT MEANS AN HEIR WAS BORN TO ISRAEL'S THRONE.
1. God promised an heir to Israel's throne; Isa. 9:6,7.
2. God will give Jesus Israel's throne; Luke 1:32.
3. God will give Him an eternal throne; Luke 1:33.

III. IT MEANS JOY WAS COME TO THE WORLD.
1. The angels rejoiced at His coming; Luke 2:13,14.
2. The shepherds rejoiced at His coming; Luke 2:20.
3. Simeon rejoiced at His coming; Luke 2:28-32.

IV. IT MEANS A SAVIOUR WAS PROVIDED.
1. He came as a ransom; Mark 10:45.
2. He came to save from sin; Matt. 1:21.
3. He came to seek and save the lost; Luke 19:10.

V. IT MEANS SATAN WOULD BE DEFEATED.
1. Christ was manifested to destroy Satan's works; I John 3:8.
2. Christ by His death destroyed Satan's works; Heb. 2:14.
3. Christ removes Satan's armor; Luke 11:21,22.

VI. IT MEANS PEACE CAN ENTER OUR HEARTS.
1. He came to bring peace; Luke 2:14.
2. He made peace on Calvary; Col. 1:20.
3. He is our Eternal Peace; Isa. 9:7.

VII. IT MEANS A WAY TO HEAVEN WOULD BE MADE.
1. A way is promised by Christ; John 14:6.
2. A way is made by God's love; John 3:16.
3. A way is made by Christ's death; Gal. 1:4.